BEYOND THE EYES

Sylvia Schenatzky

Schenatzky

2015 © Sylvia Schenatzky
ISBN-13: 978-0692355862
ISBN-10: 0692355863
Cover Credit: Kate Johannsen and
Samantha Josephine Schenatzky

TABLE OF CONTENTS

TABLE OF CONTENTS

INTRODUCTION
How I Feel About Myself

I took a deep breath and finally decided to write about what I experienced during the past year. I feel awkward and relieved at the same time about my decision to finally write this book but there is always this inner voice that says, "This is your story and everything is real – I want you to believe."

My words are exactly what have been told to me. Everything that happened to me is about a mission that has been dictated to me and I am the person chosen to execute it. The actual words I heard are "You are commanded." It began when I asked this inner voice over and over again, "Why me? Why me? I am no one." I always received the same answer, "You are the chosen one."

I am going to say it again. I am passing on the words to you just as I have received them. It is important for you to know from the bottom of my heart that I am not crazy. I am not someone who is desperate for attention or in need of pursuing money or riches. In fact, it is just the opposite. I have experienced highs and lows in my life like anyone else and have begun living life with joy. I decided to do this for someone very special. In short, it is Michael Jackson. Yes, THE Michael Jackson.

As I express my thoughts that come to mind, it seems impossible that it could be the "Greatest Entertainer of the World" or more commonly known as the "King of Pop." My personal story is almost like a nightmare that never ends. My hands start to tremble when I think about all the things that have happened to me, however, I am passing the information on the way Michael Jackson is telling me. He wants the world to know the TRUTH about what happened. This is a story of what happened between Michael and me.

It is a very tough situation for me which I am aware of, but I promised Michael I would do what he is telling me to do even though I am aware of the consequences I am facing. I told him I would do this together with him and listen to what he has to say and share with the world his heart's desire. I am alone with this tremendous task and as you can imagine, it is difficult for me to talk to anybody about my experience.

I live with fear but at the same time, curious about the development of the task at hand. I know I run the risk of being called a "nutcase", however, the fact is, I decided to write this book to demonstrate how important this experience has been with Michael and how much he has influenced my thoughts and life.

Schenatzky

CHAPTER ONE

The Reason I'm Writing This Story

After taking a deep breath, I finally decided to write about what I experienced during the past few years. I feel both awkward and a sense of enormous relief about my decision to finally write this book. An inner voice said, "This is your story, and everything is real. I want you to believe." Everything that happened to me in this story was communicated to me, and I was the person chosen to execute it. The actual words were, "You are commanded!"

It began when I asked the inner voice repeatedly, "Why me? I'm no one."

I always received the same answer. "You're the one."

The voice explained that I was the only one who could hear the message clearly and accurately. While others might pretend to communicate with the person, "You are the one I choose to communicate these messages with. It's important for you to write this book for me. My soul is very much alive. I can hear your thoughts, and you can receive my thoughts and emotions in your mind and feel them with your entire body.

"I found my love in you, and this kind of passion is still possible on the other side. I want to let people know how I felt in my life on earth, especially my love for children and my special purpose for having been in the world as a musician."

I, "Lilly," as Michael called me, pass these words on to my readers as I received them. It's important for people to know that I'm not insane. I'm not desperate for attention, nor do I pursue wealth. I'm quite the opposite. Like anyone else, my life has held highs and lows. I live a normal married life with two children and have worked in childcare for many years.

I decided to write this book because the person insists that I do it now. His name is Michael Jackson. Yes, he's *the* Michael Jackson.

It seems impossible that the voices could come from the greatest entertainer in the world, the King of Pop. I'm mandated to write these words. Michael wants us to know about his life, afterlife, gifts, soul and feelings on the other side, and what we need to do to change the direction that we, as human beings, are headed.

From what I've learned through research, Michael had spiritual inclinations. Perhaps it was natural that he chose someone who could channel his thoughts and feelings.

I knew nothing much about Michael before this experience. Like many, I enjoyed his music, but I was aware of very little that happened in his life. However, my life changed dramatically on June 25, 2009, the day he died.

I knew about his death just like everyone else, because it was on all the media. It was a big event. Strangely enough, I felt as if a close family member died. I don't know why I felt that way. It made no sense.

I had many difficulties in my life—moving away from my home in Germany, obtaining visas, almost losing everything I had in the process, and starting a new life in the United States with nothing while trying to keep my loving family together. I wasn't a religious person, but, throughout those adversities, I began telling my husband that we needed to believe that everything would work out, and we'd eventually be okay. I started praying to God for that to happen. In the process, as events unfolded and we settled into our new lives, I realized praying was something I should do more often.

At about the same time, and continuing for the next three years, I started hearing from Michael.

Sitting one night on my bedroom floor, I started crying. I missed love and felt lonely, and suddenly I realized I heard a voice for the very first time telling me he felt the same way, too, because he missed that kind of love in his life, too.

Why am I hearing this voice and who is talking to me, I wondered.

"I will love you and you will understand this love and what it means to me to have found you," came the answer. "I will tell you my name. I have passed away and I do not live in your world anymore. I need you to tell my story to get the truth out to my family and my fans. I seek you, because I have known you in previous lifetimes, and you understand me. I know this is going to be hard for you to believe, because we exist in two different dimensions."

I wondered, *Why do you need my help, and for what?* "To show the world there is an afterlife and to prove to you that you are able to hear me."

When I watched the news about the Michael Jackson case, his voice came back to me to tell me: "I want you to believe I was murdered. You're going to write a book for me. Now you know who I am. I want you to contact a medium to hear that everything I am telling you is the truth. You will be very surprised what she's going to tell you."

Later, when I consulted a professional medium, she repeatedly told me exactly the same words -- that he was murdered. The medium also told me that we shared previous lives as soul mates, and another as his sister.

On the day Michael died, my feelings of sadness and grief were so overwhelming. I prayed for him to finally find peace, as many people had done when Princess Diana died. My children were very young at the time. They saw the news of Michael's death on TV and how distraught I was.

"Mommy, are you Michael Jackson sick?"

I explained he was a famous person, and I felt I had to watch the news. I felt compelled to stay connected to the TV, as if Michael were insisting I follow all the stories about him from around the world.

As a tribute to him and to help my young daughters understand, we went outside and drew a large heart on our driveway with red sidewalk chalk. Inside we wrote, *We love you, MJ.*

I told my children Michael could see us and would know that we loved him. An enormous, deep love came over me that I still don't understand, because I knew almost nothing about him. The bright-red heart remained on our driveway through Florida rainstorms for almost a month, as if it needed to remain.

Watching the news constantly, I felt compelled to pray for Michael every night. Two weeks later, I felt his presence in our home, and I was frightened. I wanted the feeling to go away. Nervous and scared, I saw an outline of Michael sitting in the chair beside our bed and I pulled the sheets over my head. It was like seeing a transparent person, someone I recognized but also looked through.

I couldn't share my fear with anyone, even my husband. I wanted to cry and run away, but I had to live with the experience. My feelings soon became overwhelming, and I didn't know whom to turn to for help.

My hands still tremble when I think about what happened to me, but I will pass the information on the way Michael Jackson tells me. He wants the world to know the truth about what happened after he passed away, to know there's more to the afterlife than what people imagine.

He says there are other possibilities for communication and love, things no one has considered. The power of those abilities is beyond anything we can imagine. He told me that he comes into my mind as soul spirits often do with people, based on the level of my education and knowledge, skills and experiences, and my intuitive capabilities.

He said that deceased people come into the minds of the living based on what they need at the time. Love is the most powerful emotion that is communicated from the other side. That's one of the many lessons Michael Jackson wants to share with the world. He wants me to carry that message on to his family and others in the world. He claims that love is disappearing from people and is no longer a binding force.

People get married, but that love is often superficial. They make a binding commitment to God in marriage, yet they divorce almost as fast. Michael says love is the most-powerful glue holding us together. He wants this book to be written in the eyes of love, if nothing else.

"Love is the perfection and completion of all satisfaction." Those words he channeled to me sum up his idea perfectly.

How does he communicate with me? I hear his voice however it might be presented to me. Sometimes, I hear it all day, then I hear nothing for days. Sometimes, he's with me constantly throughout the night. At other times, I'll ask, "Michael, are you there? Please talk to me," but many days I don't get a response.

Once, a year passed without any communication from him. To my surprise, on October 28, he returned after exactly one year. When I wondered why he was speaking to me again, he reminded me that it was the day the movie trailer for *This Is It* came out.

He said it was the time to continue writing the book, that it was our purpose. I was awakened constantly during the night with more messages, including ones that depict his difficulties during his final tour and details of his last days, including the court case and incarceration of Dr. Murray.

Michael gives me song lyrics to write for him, yet I know nothing about music. He gives me dates and information about himself that I later verify when he tells me where to look. I always ask him for proof, and he always gives me evidence that can be confirmed.

Two years after I started writing the first draft of this book, he told me he was tired of me questioning him, asking him if he really was who he claimed. He gave me a lot of evidence and told me constantly I should "just believe," and all would be fine. If I just wrote the book and kept believing, his supreme desire would be fulfilled.

That is a tough situation that I struggle with almost every hour of the day. Michael awakens me at night with messages, because he says time doesn't exist on the other side, and he's just playing with me. He wants to talk when he feels like it. It's as if he's joking and playing as a child. He doesn't need to sleep in that dimension, so he no longer has a sleep disorder, but he was giving me one, as if he were living through me.

I promised I would do what he told me, even though I was aware of the consequences. We would do it together. I would listen to what he said, and I'd share his struggles and longings with the world. I was alone with a tremendous task, unable to talk to anyone about it, because they wouldn't understand how Michael influenced me. I often cried, and my husband and family didn't know what was wrong, as I went through the experience of being a channel for the other side. Neither did I.

I live in fear, wondering constantly how I could possibly feel the explosion of such emotions within me. I ask Michael why I feel what he does. It seems I'm living his life within me. He is simultaneously inside and outside of me, appearing in whispers and visions, a situation I can't comprehend or explain. He gives me his feelings, showing me the possibilities of what might be on the other side. His constant communication scares me, but he wants people to know it isn't frightening. He tells us a lot happens on the other side, and, in the story he communicated through me, he tells us that the deceased can see things, manipulate objects, and can even fall in love.

He also says that on the other side, souls continue to live their lives, which are predominantly of love but also have a range of mixed emotions stronger than those we experience on earth. When spirits come together on the other side, they can choose which character and emotion they wish to present to each other, and those emotions can change from moment to moment.

He explains that they can interact with those on earth in a chosen character, too. Such soul spirits are sometimes called entities, which are like big families interacting with each other. They can choose to communicate with a human being, seeing what we do. As rapidly as it happens, they can also leave or connect with another person. They can project love, hatred, or any other emotion. Within that paradigm, we, as earthly beings, can also live their lives.

As strange as it might seem, the feelings I have when I communicate with Michael feel like what we on earth experience as being deeply in love. It's difficult to verbalize the concept any other way. He gives me the emotion of almost reaching out and touching him. Michael has explained they can feel my emotions, but I can't feel theirs very much.

He also told me that he's waiting for me in his dimension, like in his song, "Waiting for You", the inspiration he gave me one day. He says we'll play like we have imagined, and only timing keeps us apart.

On one hand, the experiences of channeling Michael are frightening and disorienting, but they also feel enormously warm and loving, like the most-powerful feeling of love but deeper.

Schenatzky

Words can't express the depth of the emotion, yet there is more. It appears there are many different levels or dimension to the other side.

CHAPTER TWO
When Michael Died

When Michael died, I felt so overwhelmed with sadness and grief that I began praying for him. When my young children went outside with me to draw a large heart in our driveway with the words *We love you, MJ*, written inside, I explained that Michael could see us and would know that we love him. *You have to know the love we have for you*, I thought.

I continued to watch the news about his death and felt compelled to pray for him every night. Two weeks later, I felt his presence in our home. *Why do I feel this way?* I asked myself. *What's happening to me?*

I felt nervous and frightened. I was so afraid of my feelings, I wanted to cry and run away.

Since my husband was very busy with work, I spent a lot of time alone with my small children. One night while sitting on the bedroom floor, I burst into tears.

"I can love you," an unknown voice said. "I miss being loved." The voice became more intense. "I was murdered. I'm asking you to do something for me. You're the one."

Why am I hearing this voice? I wondered. *Am I crazy?*

"This is Michael. I was murdered." Though the voice was only a whisper, the words were clear.

"On the night of my death, I was deliberately given strong medication. It was a plan. They made me drowsy and confused, unable to respond. I heard voices around me but wasn't able to defend myself." Michael also wanted me to recount that the security system was off that night, and an unknown person had entered his home. "Even in the morning, I heard lawnmowers outside. I was still alive and semiconscious but unable to communicate with anyone. I heard my physician, Dr. Murray, taking calls on his cell phone in another room. They were his accomplices. Their intent was to murder me."

"Dr. Murray waited until my vital signs were almost gone before he dialed 911. He hadn't been checking the monitors attached to me for some time."

I received that message a few weeks after Michael's death. I was certain it was Michael Jackson, because every time I saw news stories about his death, the voice came to me.

"You understand," he said. "You can hear me. I need you to communicate the truth of what happened to me. I could predict my death, because I felt it was coming, that someone would kill me, and that's what happened. I need you to write this and let the world know the truth."

He added that an angel came to him while he was alive in the same way he came to me. The angel told him he was a special, spiritual person and always had angels around him.

I couldn't tell anyone about the voice, even my husband. If I did, he would think I was insane. The voice and the information affected my work and time with the children. I didn't know what to do.

"Please help me. I need you. You have to read my lyrics; you will find the truth in them, and you will understand." I did not really know what he meant by saying you will understand at this time. Michael said we have meet in two previous lives and that we have been soul mates. In one I was a sister. Michael said he found the love he was searching and praying for, and it would be confirmed by different mediums that I saw with Michael's guidance. He said "THIS IS IT " becomes a true story but at the time I did not know what "THIS IS IT " meant. Michael said it is a song, you will hear this song for the first time in November 2009. Michael last concert was scheduled to be "THIS IS IT", however Michael passed away on June 25, 2009. A movie was made about all of Michael's rehearsals and the song appears at the end. Michael said this would be our story.

> This is Michael Jackson. I'm still here. My soul is still alive, and I haven't passed over to the light. I can see through your eyes and hear through your ears. I can speak through your voice and mind. I can experience what you are experiencing.
>
> I'm still alive inside you, even though I know I died. We were twins, brother and sister in one previous life, and that's why you can hear me. We're connected. We can talk as easily as people on earth do.

His words stunned me. I had no way of comprehending the message, and it didn't make sense. I cried, my hands shaking. Maybe we didn't know the depth of such spirit-to-earth communication, but still, it was confusing and terrifying.

I found a magazine with Michael's picture on it and lit a candle, saying, "OK, I'll listen to you. How can I help you?"

He said I needed to write a book about him and his family, so the world could read it. The message was already clear to me what his purpose was and why he entered my life. I knew it wasn't only about the love we shared, it was much more. The world needed to know about Michael Jackson. I had never written a book; I spoke mostly German; and I didn't know how such a thing could be done.

I needed to talk to someone. Focusing on Michael's picture, I saw him wearing a silver bracelet with a symbol that resembled a turtle. Soon after that, I went to an Indian folk arts festival with my family and saw a turtle on a necklace.

"There's a turtle on the bracelet you were looking at a few days ago," Michael whispered. "It's a turtle, my totem. I've always been interested in Native American culture."

He told me many personal things, such as the movies he liked. He also liked horses, playing Hide-and-Seek, and even as an adult, he enjoyed roller coasters. He also told me very private things: how he met Dr. Murray; why his kids were home-schooled; and things that he didn't wanted me to write. Since I wasn't certain he was Michael Jackson, I asked him personal things, like when was his mother's birthday.

"May fourth."

Later, I checked that on the computer and saw that it was May fourth.

"My brother, Jermaine's, birthday is in December. The exact date is your lucky number." My lucky number is eleven. When I checked Jermaine's information on the Internet, I learned that his birthday is December eleventh.

Michael told me about his habits, like chewing his fingernails and biting his lips. Strangely enough, those habits started with me at the time of our connection. I never did those things before. Furthermore, Michael stated I walked like he did, with my thumbs in my pockets. I also laughed like him.

I checked YouTube videos of

Michael and saw that my walk and laugh were almost identical to his.

When I was at work at the childcare center one day, Michael told me he would give me more proof of his identity. He gave me the name Johnson, which I wrote on a scrap of paper.

"You'll find that name on the <u>This Is It</u> web page. Look for the coordinator first. You'll also find that name as the choreographer, and second assistant."

I didn't know what any of that meant, but, when I got home, I verified the information. The name appeared exactly as Michael said.

Another time he gave me the name David Peterson and told me to check the LAPD web site. When I got home, my husband was using the computer, so I asked him to look up the information.

"Look under administration," Michael told me. The name David Peterson was there.

"What's your connection to that name?" I asked.

"It's just more proof that you can

hear me."

I began to think the voice might really be that of Michael Jackson, though I didn't want to believe it. I was shaking.

My husband, who was more grounded, asked, "How is that possible?" I felt like it was almost Michael made a game out of this and he enjoyed doing this to me. He often tried to scare me; he said "I want you to die, I want you now! I need you here in my life." I was very afraid that Michael had the power over me to make me want to die.

I always answered, "You can't have me, Michael. I still have my life here," and Michael always answered, "I want you so badly!"

A friend of mine reads a lot of books on spiritual topics, so I finally told her about the voices. "I can hear Michael Jackson, and he wants me to write a book. When I heard that he died, I started praying for him and felt his presence in my home within days. I feel watched constantly, even when I'm in the shower. I've started turning off the lights, because I don't want him to see me naked."

I explained the things Michael said and the proof he gave me.

While I went through my daily routines with my husband and two young children, and at work at the childcare center, Michael talked to me, telling me I was the chosen one to channel his voice and experiences. He said he saw my light and knew I was a big believer, which didn't surprise me.

We painted the word *Believe* on our house. Michael said seeing that made him feel happy.

The reason we painted that word on our house had to do with moving to the United States from Germany, losing everything we had, and starting over. Believing became our family motto. We realized we had to believe that God was with us in that change. That was when I began living with joy in my heart.

Soon after we painted that word on the house, the homeowner's association said we had to remove it.

That didn't stop me. I always wanted a tattoo, and it felt like the right time. I went to a local tattoo store. Michael said when I got there, I'd recognize something I would want.

Even though I intended to have the word *Believe* tattooed on my arm, I looked at a magazine while I waited and saw Michael on the cover.

"See?" he asked. "I'm with you everywhere you go." I looked through a tattoo magazine and saw a pretty heart. "I would have loved to have one like that," Michael said. "Should the word *believe* be inside it?'

"Yes."

I soon had a permanent reminder of my family motto and Michael's choice of a heart.

Believe Tattoo

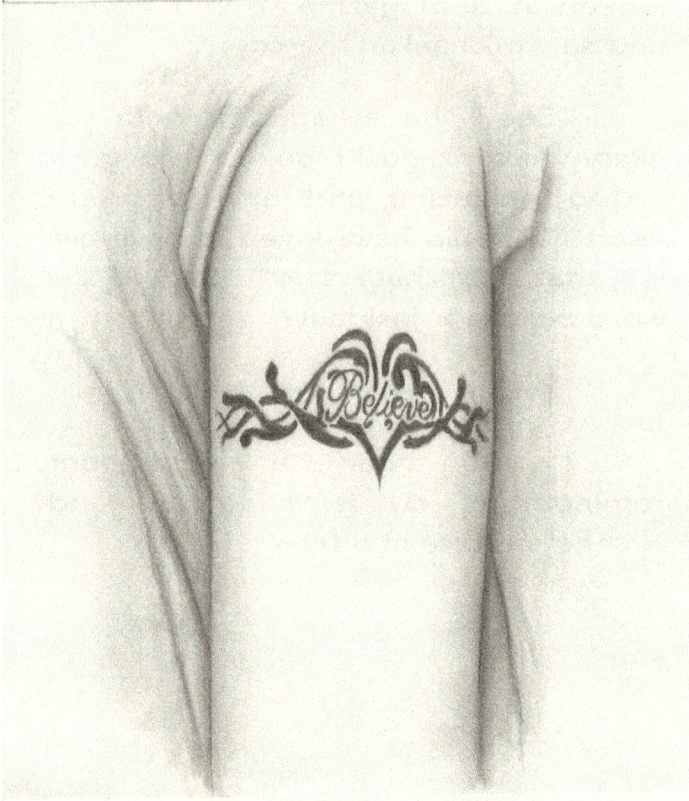

CHAPTER THREE
Michael's Memorial Service

The day of Michael's memorial service, before I heard his voice, I was scheduled to work the afternoon shift at the childcare center. I was grateful to be able to stay home and watch the service.

I lit a candle and watched. When they brought out Michael's coffin, I cried. There was a bad lightning storm outside my house, and thunder cracked. The power went off. Ever since I was a child, thunderstorms brought me strong feelings of connection and led to predictions that I didn't understand at the time, but became clear as time went on. I strongly felt this was the moment I needed to write down everything that I'd experienced.

When the power came back on again, I saw the service, where people screamed at Michael to wake up. It was so emotional, I couldn't stop crying, especially when his children, Paris and Prince Michael, stood before the microphone to speak about their father.

I went to work with swollen, puffy eyes. As I drove, I heard the song, "I Can't Stop Loving You" playing on the radio, which made it worse. I cried harder, but I forced myself to continue to work.

"What happened to you?" people asked when I arrived.

It was a horrible day. I never cried so much in my life. That strong emotional feeling pulled at my heart. I never felt anything so powerful before.

CHAPTER FOUR
Psychic Connections

I came from a large family in a small town in Battenberg, Germany, with six siblings. I was the fifth child, what some would have called the troubled child. I grew up in a big house with a big family, but it wasn't until I was nine years old that I predicted things that might occur and saw people who had passed.

A few months before my father's death, he was ill but didn't know how sick he was. One day as I stood by the window looking out at the ground, I saw a tall, thin man wearing a black robe with a black hood over his head: Death. He looked up and smiled at me, saying my father would die soon. My father and I were very close, so the news terrified me.

Another time, I had a vision that one of the ducks living in the pond a few miles from our house would die. I told my mother about it, and she went. Sure enough, the duck was dead. I realized I could connect with or predict death, but I was still a young child I knew I was different from other kids. I told my mother what would happen next, with specific details, and those things always came true. No one made me feel weird or strange for this ability. It was accepted as my gift.

Before we moved to our current house in Florida, I knew someone had died there, which our next-door neighbor confirmed. When I was in my early twenties, I told my husband I was continuously obsessed with the thought that I would be connected to someone famous someday, though I had no idea who it might be or why it would happen.

In February 2009, when I was in my forties, I received a strong prediction and the image of a famous man who would die. The thought came to me that I'd be connected to him in the afterlife, though I didn't tell anyone.

CHAPTER FIVE
Unusual Experiences

One morning, I was eating breakfast when Michael came to me and said he would always find a way to talk to me. He told me I was his tool, and, as I sat there, my hands moved automatically, as if some strong energy could move them without my conscious desire.

"What are you doing to me?" I asked.

"I can manipulate you in many ways. This is just one example." He could also move his personal energy into my body when we listened to music. One night, I lay in bed listening to his song "I Can't Stop Loving You", when Michael moved my hand to the melody, as if I were conducting the tune. His energy flowed into my hands to the rhythm perfectly, making various shapes. I found exactly these shapes on video to this song what he used to do with his hands when he performed. My hands also moved automatically when we listened to "Believe" by Josh Groban from *The Polar Express* soundtrack. It was like art—magical.

Before a Halloween party for the soccer organization my husband founded, I was in a store looking for a pirate costume to match my husband's. I found a cute one and thought it was perfect.

I began paying for it, but I suddenly became so dizzy, I almost fainted, losing control of my body. I had to leave the costume and get out of the store.

Once I returned to my car, I was fine.

"I wanted you to honor me again by looking like me," Michael explained, "with a silver arm band and glittered silver glove. I didn't want you to wear that pirate costume."

Angry and stunned, I ended up wearing my second choice, a vampire costume. That incident was typical of the manipulations that occurred over several years. They never seemed to stop.

At another Halloween party scheduled for the members of the Florida soccer club, I told Michael I wanted to honor him that year at the party, so I chose a military jacket like his, a glittered glove, and anything else I could find that Michael wore when he was alive.

My husband arranged the party for the kids, and they were excited. A few days before, Michael told me, "Something will happen at the party."

We hired a group of dancers from the high school as part of the entertainment. Before we left the house to go to the party, Michael said, "When the dancers start performing their dance to "Thriller", the power will go off."

Since it was 8:00 at night, it was already dark out. The performers were going through "Thriller" when the power died.

Oh, my goodness, I thought. Michael told me this would happen during the performance.

I was shocked. How could that have happened? I looked at my friend, and we stared in amazement. The power came on again, and the party continued, but I was so terrified, I ended up in the hospital, thinking I'd gone insane.

An examination didn't find anything unusual, so I was checked out of the hospital and went home. I woke at 3:00 AM and saw a round, bright light moving up and down on the right side of the bedroom wall. I never saw anything like it before. Michael told me it was his light.

One day later, my eight-year-old daughter woke up and came from her room. She saw the same round light moving up and down on her bedroom wall. The circle was clear and perfect, not blinding, and it appeared off and on in my home for weeks.

Months later, my husband and I saw a similar white light but even brighter in our bedroom. The flat, horizontal, elongated light moved quickly through the room and to the ceiling. The windows were closed, and it was dark out, but the light was clearly in the room. Soon it disappeared.

Michael did some scary things to me that I wasn't always aware of. I didn't realize he was giving me his bad habits, one of which was biting my lip, which I did for several weeks. He later told me he gave those habits to me. I thought that was very unusual.

He told me I could see for myself and sent me to a web page that showed an interview he had with Oprah Winfrey at Neverland. When I watched the 1997 interview, I saw him continuously bite his lip. Michael said that was when Oprah asked if he was a virgin, which embarrassed him.

Such strange experiences were disconcerting.

Michael also said he didn't eat pork because of his religion. I always liked pork, because I came from Germany. Suddenly, I couldn't eat it anymore. MJ influenced many things in my life.

One night we were eating dinner at the kitchen table, and suddenly, I felt Michael move my index finger to my lip. His energy was very strong. I asked why he was doing such things to me. Since I usually did what he asked, that was probably why he kept sharing energy with me.

He could make me do things without my being aware of it. During an interview with Martin Brashear in a video about living with Michael, I saw Martin bring his index finger to his lips. Michael told me that it would be shown.

I went on my computer, and Michael told me where to find the exact part.

Such things happened often. I felt like Alice in Wonderland, but it was real. Michael showed me private videos and was able to tell me exactly what came next. I felt as if I were taking part in a mind game with him and other entities. I wanted to find the key to the game to understand who was doing it to me.

One day, I was in the laundry room, and Michael said the washer would stop working, and it did. He did such things frequently.

The incredible emotions he gave me were amazing, too. One day I was shopping at Target for my daughter's birthday. Michael told me I had to believe him, and, while I was in the middle of the store, he gave me incredible emotions that were impossible to describe. He could give me such feelings no matter where I was.

Schenatzky

48

CHAPTER SIX
Curious and More Curious

I wondered why Michael referred to me as Lilly, so I asked him. He said the name reminded him of a little girl he saw occasionally at Neverland. She gave him inspiration for life. "Now you're giving me inspiration, so I want to call you Lilly," he said. I liked it and agreed.

I was curious how he got his inspiration for music and lyrics. He told me he woke from dreams and started writing. The process was interesting to him, because he heard the words, and everything appeared before his face. That was something he seemed to channel through me, too.

Most people think when they die, they are just dead. Michael wants us to know the truth, that there was more.

The biggest question I asked him

many times was, "How do you exist in the dimension you're communicating from?"

He came to me in many different voices, sometimes warm and familiar, sometimes like his regular human voice, and sometimes in a distant whisper.

"What's your being like?" I asked.

He said he lived but didn't need to eat, sleep, or use the bathroom. The soul is nothing but energy. It can take the form of a human body. When the body dies, all that's left is energy, which can enter a living body and possess it, creating a vehicle to speak, see, and hear through that person.

I know there are those who are trapped between dimensions, and even Michael was confused about how that happened. What we didn't know with certainty was what happened when a person died and went into the light. Michael thought that would keep occurring until he passed over. Since he could possess my body, he lived my life with my family and me.

With his energy, Michael wanted to play and go on adventures at any time of the night. Time didn't exist for him. He often woke me in the middle of the night and whispered, "I want to play with you. Come on an adventure with me."

Since I was awake and in his mind, I sent him an image of doing things he loved, like going to Disneyland and playing together. He told me he was Peter Pan at heart and could fly, while I was his Tinker Bell.

In our imagination, we played. The feelings were as if we were together as children. I had to initiate the adventure in my mind.

Communication was easier when I listened to music. Michael always wanted me to listen to music, so I plugged in my MP3 player, and we had fairytale adventures in our minds. I used his music a lot, but almost any music was good for those nightly activities. We felt emotions based on the choice of songs.

When I listened to vocal music through my MP3 player, Michael's energy came through the player and made the voices higher or lower, manipulating the electrical waves with his energy.

He comes to me in many different ways and forms. He said that if we were together on earth as a married couple, he would make me more valuable, we would have a lot of fun giggling, watching funny movies until we fell asleep, laughing, eating ices and candy, and climbing trees.

He said he found a love in me that he always wanted, and showed me through his songs because it would make more sense to me. It made me always cry. Both felt we were kids in an adult body, but we were in another dimension and couldn't have that love. We feel almost overly connected and are enormously dependent on each other. We'll have to wait for another lifetime to be completely connected.

At that time, he inspired me to write the following lyrics.

<u>Waiting for You</u>

Remember the things we used to do

The way we fell for each other

Beyond The Eyes

The way we stared into each other's eyes

Oh, Baby, I can't wait

I can't wait

Falling for you again

Take me to a place

Where no one has been before

I wanna touch you

I wanna feel your lips

I wanna discover a new way to love you

Oh, Baby, I can't wait

I can't wait

Falling for you again

It feels like it takes too long to feel this

love again,

Schenatzky

Let me be your obsession

Oh, Baby, I can't wait

I can't wait

Falling for you again

We acted like kids

Climbing up trees on a beautiful summer day

We chased each other across the meadow

We watched funny movies and laughed till we fell asleep

I was holding your hands

All I said is, I want you, Baby, I can't wait

Oh, Baby, I can't wait

I can't wait

Falling for you again

When your time on earth is through

I will be there for you

Oh, Baby, I can't wait

I can't wait

Falling for you again

Michael has given me many lyrics and inspired my thoughts, though I have absolutely no experience with songwriting, music, or poetry. It surprises me each time it happens. I just sit down, and it quickly comes to mind. I try to notate what he says as rapidly as it comes to me. My English isn't strong enough for such lyrical language to be mine. It's clearly coming from someplace above, and it stuns me each time it happens.

I keep asking myself, "How is this even possible?" The first set of lyrics was called The Truth, which details the truth about Michael and his life on earth, a life of tragedy. Much of what happened to him when he was alive is in that song. He told me "Be aware of Robert and in time you will know." Years later, the contents of the following lyrics were confirmed by a video I found on YouTube. In it, a federal agent named Robert declared that Michael was truly murdered.

<u>The Truth</u>
Now he appears to be carefree

But the mystery needs to be uncovered

He has been a victim of a crime

The power prevails

He was pursued and chased
They did what they wanted
The truth is still hidden
The "KKK?" Snedden

That is what they wanted
But then what a world of racism

Oh no, oh no, oh no, oh no,

*We miss the songs he used to sing
to us
We miss the songs he used to sing
to us
We miss the songs he used to sing
to us*

*When he's dead
You all watch his videos
And listen to his songs
But who really understood his
lyrics?*

*He was sent forth
For healing the world
And his love for the children*

*Some people really loved him
But some people just say it
Then why don't you say the truth?
That you were one of the people
Who always insulted him
The minute he started breaking
all-time records
Elvis records and Beatle records*

*They called him a freak
A homosexual
Child molester and he was
bleaching his skin
They did everything to turn the
public against him
But we must achieve*

Schenatzky

We must seek truth in all things

We miss the songs you used to sing to us
We miss the songs you used to sing to us
We miss the songs you used to sing to us

Michael told me the book would be published first, then someone who read it would find me and help compose music to some of his lyrics. I don't know anyone in the music business and wouldn't have a clue where to start. Michael wants the world to know he'll inspire someone to write the music. One of the mediums I eventually consulted confirmed someone would do that, though I still don't know who.

Months later, my husband was in Jacksonville for work and happened to speak to someone whose job used to be composing music for Nickelodeon and was currently working for Disney World. Later, my husband contacted him and asked if he could show him something.

The person didn't know about my experiences but was willing to look at the lyrics. My husband showed him The Truth and asked him what he thought, wondering how good they were without giving him any more information. "This sounds like something Michael Jackson would have written," the man said.

Other friends I've shown the lyrics have said the same thing. They say the words are powerful, and they sound vaguely like Michael Jackson.

Schenatzky

CHAPTER SEVEN
Love and Tragedy with Children

Unfortunately, Michael's love for children became a nightmare, because he was accused of molesting children. He simply wanted to be an inspiration to them and to have them like his music. Their approval, Michael told me, meant more to him than anything else.

"When I had kids around me, I found things I never had in my own life," Michael said. "I was filled with happiness, but very often, I cried from loneliness. I wanted to be loved by people all around the world, but I especially wanted to be loved by children. Life without children would be a life without love."

As I wrote this book, he told me, "The worst thing they did to me was bring me up on child molestation charges and make money from my popularity."

Michael claims he was so emotionally devastated that he wrote a song about Tom Snedden for his fans, which he called DS. Michael told me we would find the song on his history album, which is connected to the Truth song.

Michael's purpose was to stop the world of racism. The world needs to know it's time for a change to give black people the respect they deserve. It has to stop!

Mirror Reflection   Childhood Memories

CHAPTER EIGHT
Reflections and Realizations

Wherever I went, Michael sent me hearts to remind me of our special connection. That happened once at my work place. I work with children in a local day care center inside a gym. One day, a little girl drew a picture of a heart on a piece of paper and handed it to me.

"That's your heart," Michael told me. Everything is true. You have to believe me. You can hear me. You understand and get my inspiration. You are blessed.

Anytime I listened to music, it brought a beautiful wave of love. I was living in his world, not on earth. I spent more and more time with him, using any free time I had, and I felt an incredible feeling of love.

He told me he was falling, and I was deeply in love with him. Even later, when I began working on the book, the feeling came to me, and I interpreted that as his way of thanking me.

I realized what was happening to me was very unusual. I was falling in love with someone who wasn't there. He was present in spirit, and I was in love with him. I acted like he was my real life and really existed. I was able to see and feel him. We laughed and played with each other like kids. Michael "said you made me feel so real"

My husband thought I was having an affair and was so jealous he wanted to kick me out of the house.

"Are you in love with someone else?" he asked bluntly. I didn't know how to explain, but I tried to make him understand.

Every day, I wrote in my notebook what happened. I had no idea what I would write, but I wrote down anything and everything that came to me. Many times, it didn't make sense, but I wrote it, anyway.

Michael gave me more evidence that he was real and wanted me to believe that what was happening between us was true. He told me what would happen ahead of time. Since then, I've experienced many cases of déjà vu, as if situations had happened before. That happened even with people and things I had no connection with. He always liked Christmas with his friend, Elizabeth Taylor, because she made him happy by the wonderful ways she decorated his house. Michael told me to get a video on the computer to see the beautiful decorations.

I knew nothing about that, but he was right. When revelations like that happened, I cried.

Schenatzky

CHAPTER NINE

Letter to Liz

In October 2009, two weeks before it came out, Michael told me I would see a headline on the front page of newspaper that read "Liz Taylor Has 3 Months to Live". While I waited in line at the grocery store, I saw a magazine called Globe Exclusive dated October 26, 2009, with the headline in bold:

Liz Taylor Has 3 Months to Live

Michael asked me to write a letter to Liz Taylor, his longtime friend. I thought receiving such a letter might give her a heart attack, because Michael was dead.

"Don't worry about it," he told me.

"I won't do it."

"Yes, you will." He was very persistent.

"How will I find out where she

lives? How will she know it comes from you?"

"Tell her it's from an angel."

I finally agreed.

Writing a letter to Liz Taylor sounded ridiculous, but I tried, anyway. Michael said her favorite color was purple, and I needed purple stationery. He wanted me to write something that reminded him of his life as a performer and how he felt. A part of this was already written by Smokey Robinson, but he wanted me to use it. I also did some adding to it.

The letter was like a poem and came automatically through my thoughts and hand much like Michael's lyrics.

Coming from an angel

Now if I appear to be carefree

It's only to camouflage my sadness

In order to shield my pride

I try to cover this hurt with a show
    of gladness

But don't let my show convince you

That I have been happy since you
    decided to go

Oh, I need you so

The immortality is a mystery

It seems like painful shots

And a dividing line between us

I'm heard

I want you to know

Oh, I miss you so

If I can comfort you

Don't be afraid

When you feel my arms on your
shoulders

I found her address on the
Internet, and Michael asked me to
place a picture of an angel on the
outside of the envelope. Michael loves
angels and always had many in his
home.

On the way to the post office, Michael told me he would send me a song.

You have to turn on the radio to hear it. He did things like that often. You'll hear the song, "Rock With You (All Night)". I'm so happy you're doing this for me.

I sent the letter by certified mail. After seven days without a confirmation, I wondered what happened. My husband and I called the Beverly Hills Post Office and asked someone to track it.

I described the envelope.

"It's right here in front of me," the woman said. "It has an angel on it. I know Liz personally and will deliver it directly to her."

Though I had my return address on the envelope, I never knew if Liz read the letter.

Beyond The Eyes

Schenatzky

CHAPTER TEN
Deciding to Write

I told my friend, Elizabeth, about what happened to me, and she suggested I see a medium, which sounded like a good idea.

The experiences were coming too fast to comprehend. My town had a place where a person could get an inexpensive reading from a medium each week, so I decided to check.

The moment I walked inside, one medium said, "Your life is about to change. You'll write a book."

"Write a book? Me? What about?" I didn't know what she meant.

A different medium approached me and said, "It will be very personal. One day, people will believe you and your story."

Another lady came up. "You have a lot of questions about an entity you're connected to."

I felt confused and depressed.

"This entity died at the age of fifty and was very handsome. He's channeling you and wants your help. Don't be afraid. He saw your light, which is why he was able to find you. He was searching for you."

I felt cold and frightened. They were talking about Michael Jackson.

I wanted to tell my husband, but I knew he would tell me to forget about it, because it was too crazy. I told my girlfriend exactly what the medium at the center said, and she warned me to be very careful.

I saw other mediums each week, and they said the same thing. I didn't know what my friend meant when she said to be careful.

I went to bed and lit a candle, praying to God for understanding and clarity. Overwhelmed by what was happening, I needed to understand what "being careful" meant.

My mind was filled with questions and confusion. How could I hear such an entity, and why was it coming to me in such a way? How would it influence my life? Family and friends were concerned about me. Michael's communication consumed me day and night.

In September 2009, I decided to visit another medium with my friend, Elizabeth. The professional medium's name was also Elizabeth, and she had over twenty years' experience in her field.

My friend knew I was nervous about what the medium might say, so she accompanied me. I sat in the car and listened to Michael tell me how surprised I would be by what the medium would say.

"Everything I've told you is true. You just have to believe it's true. The medium will tell you the same things I've said."

My hands shook as we walked toward Elizabeth's office for my reading. She invited me to sit down and remain calm. I never met her before, and she knew nothing about me. She asked me to listen and not ask any questions yet, and she told me not to tell her any personal information about myself.

She immediately felt the eyes of a

male and said I was in touch with an entity who'd been murdered. "The eyes are everywhere," she added.

"There were millions of dollars involved in his death. Something happened to his head in 1984, with his hair and skull, as if there were a fire."

I knew she meant the Pepsi commercial Michael did when his hair caught fire.

"He was fifty years old, and his skin color changed from a skin disorder." She did automatic writing on a piece of paper. The message read, "This is Michael Jackson talking to you. I love you very much. You're a special person to me."

"He wants you to believe what you hear and to write a book about him. He calls you Lilly. You are his Lilly. He asks you to believe everything he tells you. He is telling me you wanted to have a tattoo on your arm with the word Believe. He's happy you did it, because it will protect you in the future."

I didn't know why she said that or how it might protect me. "Debbie is the mother of his two children."

I knew very little about Michael's life and only discovered that the medium told the truth much later. I was almost in tears with shock.

How can I be Lilly? I wondered. My name's Sylvia. Write a book about Michael Jackson? I have no experience writing anything. My English is poor, because my native language is German.

"You'll find someone to help you with this project," the medium said. "It will come out in two years. The story will be like a volcano to you. You'll work on it with three people.

"You will also write songs for him."

I almost laughed. "I don't know how to write, and I certainly don't know anything about music."

"You'll do it. You'll write the truth about Michael Jackson's life." I wanted to run. I didn't want to do what she said or be involved in any way. It was too dangerous. Michael was a world-renowned entertainer. Even though I knew little about his life, I understood he was an international celebrity, while I was just a homemaker and childcare worker.

"You'll be fine," she said. "Michael likes the fact that Lilly works with children, because he was fond of them himself."

She did more automatic writing. " I have been searching for you all my life, because you were my sister in a past life."

"When he died," she said, "he couldn't find you right away. When you started praying for him, he saw your light."

"He doesn't want to go into the light yet. He wants to protect and guide his children. He wants you to finish this project for him. He wants the truth to be known about his life and death and how he felt about it. He'll give you some lyrics and facts to include in the book. He has already given you four sets of lyrics that you were inspired to write. He wants you to know he'll give you a secret code to prove all of this is real." As the medium said, those were lyrics I wrote. That was very strange, because I didn't write poetry and certainly not in English.

I never wrote music or lyrics before, so I found it highly unusual I was able to write them. I wondered why I felt inspired to do that, because it wasn't something I would have attempted in a language I didn't know well.

Elizabeth wrote two words, *Cool Move.*

"What does that mean?" I asked.

"I don't know. Those words will come from him sometime in the near future. At that time, you'll know everything is true. The words will come to you in a few weeks. He's telling you to believe him."

She gave me the names of my family members, which Michael told her, and she wrote them on a piece of paper. "Your mom's name is Margaret."

"Oh, my God. That's right." I was stunned. She wrote, *Christa.*

"Yes. My sister's name is Christa."

She didn't know me at all, and she would not have known the names of my family members.

"Michael can see everything and knows what will happen in the future. It's like the movie Ghost."

Since I'd seen the movie, I began to understand a little of what she said.

"You are blessed. Don't be scared. Everything will be fine. He's using you to write his lyrics. Be careful to write down everything Michael gives you."

"The lyrics will be successful. You'll find someone who'll compose the music for them, but the book will come out first. Then people will believe you more when they read your story, and they know it comes directly from MJ. In fact, everything he has given you is absolutely truthful."

The last thing she said before I left was, "Michael loves your outfit and loves Germany very much. Just trust him."

I hugged my friend, Elizabeth. With tears in my eyes, I said, "This is so crazy. How do I handle this? I really can hear him."

I was so nervous and frightened, I couldn't go home. I suggested we stop at Starbucks for coffee. As we sat in Starbucks, all I could do was cry. "How can this happen to me?" I asked my friend. "I'm nobody. How can I write a book?"

"Apparently you were his sister in a past life. What's meant to be is meant to be."

I had nothing but questions. On the way home, I asked Michael to please help and protect me and not leave me until my questions were answered.

Suddenly, I realized for the first time what kind of love I felt, and I questioned those feelings, too.

When I was home, I sat on the couch. Michael wanted me to close my eyes. He showed me angels that looked as if they were connected by touching each other's fingers. He also pointed out a picture, which I could see in my mind, of Michael wearing his red shirt black pants holding kids to his left and right. He said that he loved this picture.

I made an appointment with another medium and asked my husband to come with me. It seemed better for her to explain things to him, because I knew he thought I was crazy.

The medium told him his wife wasn't crazy and would write a book about MJ. She said it was really happening. We were married for twenty years, and he tried to believe me.

"Michael knows your wife from a past life," she said. "He gives her lyrics to write for him. He wants your wife to believe him and to prove to you this is really happening."

"When you go to work today, you'll hear a song on the radio from Michael called "You Are Not Alone". You have to believe and know this is from Michael."

My husband drove to Jacksonville, Florida, for work that day. She told him Michael would send him a song on the radio precisely at 3:00 PM. "Please turn on the radio at that time and listen to it."

Michael did the same thing to me all

the time, but that time, he did it to my husband.

After our session, I went home with my friend for a cup of coffee. My husband called on his way to Jacksonville. At 3:00, he pulled over and said he had to call me back, because he couldn't talk at that moment.

I knew something was wrong. Finally, he called me back. "The song came on the radio at three o'clock like the medium said."

When my husband arrived home at 10:30 that night, he asked, "How can this possibly happen?"

October 23, 2009, was my birthday, and I decided to schedule a second visit to the medium named Elizabeth. I brought my friend Elizabeth, with me. She always offered great comfort before, during, and after my visits to the medium.

"It's time to write the book," the medium said. "The title will be This Is It. The picture on the cover will be golden-looking eyes. It will be a story about Michael Jackson and Lilly."

"I don't want to get involved with this," I said. "I'm still questioning what you say." I felt nervous. All I really wanted was for my husband to understand what was going on and for me to be the kind of mother to my girls I'd been in the past.

The unusual experiences came more rapidly. I meditated often, using a candle with a wonderful floral scent. The medium told me Michael would send me the scent of almonds, which left me very confused. How could a deceased person send a smell? Voices I could understand, but a smell?

A few days later when I arrived home from work, I found a package from Germany waiting for me from my sister. Inside was a box of almond tea. I was stunned. How could that be?

It was a frightening time for me. Each time I visited the medium, Elizabeth, she gave me another piece of the puzzle. During one visit, she told me what the book cover should look like, with just Michael's eyes on the front. The letters should be gold.

"Michael wants a special part of the book to include his shoes with his socks on the lower-left corner. The gloves should be on the other side."

Michael was very specific about the book's appearance. I wrote down his instructions without knowing what I would write about in the book itself.

Other pieces of evidence that the situation was real, and the book had to be written, came in, and I told the medium.

One day, Michael told me I'd meet someone named William with a big tattoo. He said that person had a big heart.

I was nervous about that, but Michael repeated it, so I had to believe him. The next day when I went to work, I met a new woman scheduled to work with me that day. I'd never seen her before. She wore shorts with a big tattoo on her leg with the name William on it.

"What does the tattoo mean?" I asked.

"My grandmother's last name was William. She had a big heart. She was a great person, so I wanted to memorialize her."

How is this possible? I wondered. The medium said this would happen. I almost told the woman about my experiences with the medium, but I didn't. I felt she'd just think I was crazy.

"Now I'm telling you," Michael told me. "You have to write the book for me. I'll help you and support you with everything."

"Before the book is published, it will appear twice in the newspapers. One article will be in a Los Angeles paper. The editorial staff will make fun of the "This Is It" lyrics and will say the author probably wrote them herself. That will be a misunderstanding. All you will do is interpret the lyrics already published by someone else.

"The other article will be very positive and will be in a Boston newspaper. Your life will change. It will be your hardest challenge."

I went home and told my husband and two little girls I would write a book about Michael Jackson, and that was that.

My husband looked at me for a while. "If we hadn't been married over twenty years, I would think you're completely crazy."

"I can give you the medium's phone number. You can call her and verify what I just told you."

"That's not necessary. I believe you."

I felt relieved, and my fear vanished. I couldn't sleep that night, and my husband and I talked for hours in bed. It felt so good to finally tell him what was happening to me.

On another of my three visits to see Elizabeth, the medium, I asked, "Do you remember giving me the secret code *Cool Move*?"

Michael's movie trailer was due to come out October 28, 2009. The medium said that when I heard those words, I would know it was all true.

"You'll hear it from his own mouth. Don't worry that you'll miss it. You'll hear it when you're supposed to."

One day while I cleaned house, I had the TV on. I saw Michael's movie trailer. He stood at the PA system wearing a black jacket with a silver bar, as he pointed his finger at something.

I sat on the couch to watch.

"Cool move," he said. "Cool move."

"Oh, my God!" I ran to my husband to tell him what just happened. I was speechless and so overwhelmed, I cried. The medium told me it would happen the first time I met her in September. I saw the trailer in October.

I finally realized Michael was pointing at the dance moves Kenny Ortega showed him while they talked on TV.

I will always remember that day. I had trouble sleeping that night, because I couldn't believe that it happened just the way the medium said. I'd been waiting for that moment a long time.

At another of our sessions, Elizabeth told me, "Michael will give you a present soon."

"What could he possibly give me?" I asked.

"I have no idea."

When Michael's movie came out in November 2009, I wanted to see it very badly. I called my friend Elizabeth to go with me. I was very excited.

The atmosphere in the theater was beautiful. People wore things Michael would have worn, like his hats, T-shirts, and jackets.

We watched the movie. At the end, as we began to leave, a song played. "Stay and listen," Michael told me. I sat down. "Listen carefully. This is your present. Remember what the medium told you? This is your present from me."

It didn't make sense, but I stayed to listen. The song was "This Is It".

When I went home, Michael asked me to print out the lyrics so I could read them carefully. As I read them three times, suddenly, a feeling came over me. I knew what kind of book I would write. I remembered the first words Michael told me in the beginning "THIS IS IT becomes a true story." It would be Michael's story channeled through me about what happened to him in the afterlife and our special relationship.

I had no idea how I would write a book and felt no one would believe me. Michael assured me I was wrong. He would help people to believe my story.

The lyrics to "Believe "say it all.

That was how I finally decided to write a book. I didn't know where to start, so I went on the Internet to look for writers. I found one person, SG, who wrote a first, general draft of a few of my experiences.

Then I found Kate Johannsen, my daughter's art teacher, to be my illustrator. I found MS, an English teacher and writer in my town, who would become my main writer and editor.

Through it all, Michael said he was humbled by my grace, because writing the book meant so much to him. Michael pointed out a song to me called "Speechless". He wanted me to listen to it because it contains the truth about what happened to him after he passed away. I was stunned.

CHAPTER ELEVEN
Mediumship Classes

I finally decided to attend some ongoing mediumship classes so I could learn more about what was happening to me. Before the first session, Michael said he'd give me a code for his name so I would know he was with me at the class.

The class met once a week, with ten to fifteen people. It was a place to share experiences with other people and talk to those who had passed away. Michael loved Peter Pan, so he told me that when I received a message from him during class, he would use the name Peter. He felt he had Peter Pan in his heart. No one else would know Peter was actually Michael Jackson. He didn't want to use his real name, because people would ask too many questions.

When I attended class, I found that the other people had the same experiences I'd been having for some time. It was comforting to know others had similar stories to mine, and I wasn't alone.

However, my experiences were different from theirs in many ways. During class, we removed a personal item like a ring, bracelet, or watch, and placed them in a basket. Each person took an item from the basket, and we learned how to read each other by holding the item in our hands. We said whatever came to mind while we held the item.

A woman held a special coin from Germany, much like the coin my mother gave me, which had an angel on it. My mother told me not to lose it, because it would bring good luck.

The woman added that a male voice was coming through. It was someone named Peter, who loved me very much. I was going to write his book.

"You know why he's using the name Peter, because he's very close to you," she added.

I was stunned.

Schenatzky

CHAPTER TWELVE

A Session with Sandra, an Experienced Medium

Sandra, a medium, holds sessions in her home. She is very experienced and has worked with the police in solving cases.

The first thing she mentioned was four nights prior to our session, Michael visited her. She said his energy was very strong, and she knew who he was immediately.

"Michael knew we'd be seeing you," I said. "That's why he made a point to visit you beforehand."

My husband came with me. We sat at a table in Sandra's home.

"Michael's spirit is very strong," Sandra said. "He knew when he was going to die, and that he wouldn't go to the other side easily."

The following are the major points from my session with Sandra and reflect different parts of our conversation. They are disjointed, as visits to a medium often are.

1. Michael liked Sandra. When he visited her, he showed her the lyrics of his song about saving trees, which he said was on the *This Is It* album. Then Michael told her he knew he was going to die.

2. At first, she didn't know what he was talking about, so she went to buy the movie. She knew that the message was connected to me, though. Michael told Sandra about me before I called to arrange a session. When Michael first died, he told Sandra, "To be God." He told her of the past life I shared with Michael, too.

3. Michael appeared to Sandra more like a Native American, not how he looked in his lifetime, which was one reason why he wanted to change his appearance. One day, Michael showed her a blanket and repeated the word to her, but she didn't know what he meant.

4. I told her how overwhelmed I was with the situation and how Michael always asked me to believe in what he said. He always told me I worried too much. The book would be a true story.

5. My husband told Sandra of his experience showing the lyrics to a composer who worked as an independent songwriter for Disney World. The writer said the lyrics seemed as if someone who was Native American wrote them. Sandra replied that was how Michael visited her, as a Native American.

6. The composer at Disney World said the lyrics sounded like something Michael Jackson would write. My

husband asked why he would say that, and he said he was forty- seven and grew up with Michael's music. Finally, my husband told the writer about my connection with Michael. Since he was a composer, he could see how the lyrics were written by a songwriter.

7. I pointed out to Sandra that Michael told me to write the lyrics for him. "It's almost like he isn't going away anytime soon," Sandra said. The song "This Is It" is a story about what happened to me. Even though she hadn't heard the song, I told her when I first saw a medium, she told me Michael would give me a secret code with the words "Cool move". Michael told me that as soon as I heard the song "Blue Moon", I would know everything that happened was true.

8. Michael told me I would understand soon. One day when I worked at home with the TV on, I saw Michael standing at a podium. He pointed a finger at something I didn't

see and said, "Cool move," twice. I was shocked, but that was how Michael said I would know everything that happened was true.

9. I told Sandra that I had no interest in having a tattoo, but Michael insisted it would protect me. I described the festival I went to and remembered thinking how I loved the word *Believe*. Even though I didn't like tattoos, I decided to have one.

10. My husband described his road trip, where he would be in the car for two hours on business. He tried very hard to be realistic, steadfast, and not become involved in what was happening to me, but he remained open. He believed it was true. When he saw Jermaine and LaToya interviewed on TV, they were asked if they knew what the song "This Is It" meant, and neither had any idea.

11. I explained that his father was interviewed many times on TV, but he had no clue what Michael was

Schenatzky

talking about in that song. I pointed out that when the lyrics said, "I have known you for a thousand years," I felt his presence. The lyrics also said, "You don't want me here." That was true. I had no interest in any of the situation, much less Michael.

12. Sandra understood how persistent spirits could be, but I still didn't know why I could see and feel Michael's presence. I knew I was gifted and saw future events. Michael came to me, because he knew I could do those things. I told her about my experience with a woman who died in our present home. That was when I realized I was connected to the spirit world, but it really began when Michael came to me.

13. Sandra pointed out that Michael chose me because he knew I was gifted and not a particularly big fan of his. I could feel him doing things, and I told my husband that Michael

100

followed me around and did scary things to me.

14.   I felt it was important to tell Sandra that Michael gave me his habits. She said that meant he was close to me and was actually in my energy space. It was like he was attached to me. That happened to her, too. She shared a story about a man who was obsessed with her and didn't want her dating other men. When they came over, he threw things at them. That freaked them out, and they left, because they didn't want anything to do with her.

15.   I told her he kept trying to get me into his mind, because he wanted me to feel what he felt. He shared emotional thoughts with me. I mentioned that when I was having CAT scans in the hospital, Michael told me not to worry. Everything would be fine.

16.   Sandra pointed out that when Michael visited her one week before our meeting, he showed her a

tattoo on his chest that was in a different language from his past life as a Native American. He had those tattoos then, and he carried them over into this life with the Native-American words for *love* and *believe*.

17. Michael had a heart on his chest with the word *believe* inside. I told Sandra that on the way to the tattoo store, Michael told me I'd see a picture of his face at the store. I saw a magazine with his photograph on it. When I told Michael he had to stay with me, he replied, "Of course I am. I'm always with you. I'll help you choose the tattoo." I had no idea what kind of tattoo I would choose. Michael said he'd help as I flipped through the pages of a tattoo book. You'll know it when you see it. I found it and loved it.

18. When the situation with Michael began, he sent me hearts all the time. Wherever I went, I saw hearts. Once he told me I'd receive a letter from Germany with a heart in it.

When it arrived, I saw a big heart on the first page. "You see? You have to believe," Michael said. He sent me songs on the radio. When I drove to Wal-Mart, he told me to turn on the radio so I could hear *Rock With You (All Night)*. It always happened. I told him I wished he knew how that felt to me— scary and nice simultaneously.

19. Sandra pointed out that Michael wanted me to believe him. We realized that the lyrics were important to Michael, because they shared his feelings. At that moment, I decided to write the book. I felt I had no choice and was struck by waves of feeling horrible and anxious. Sandra said that was quite common among mediums. Every time she went to a place that had lots of activity, she had an anxiety attack.

20. I told her how I often felt Michael walking beside me, as if he were touching me. His emotions became mine.

Schenatzky

Sandra asked if I ever felt worn out or tired after a visit from Michael, and I said, "Yes, in more ways than one." Sandra pointed out spirits feed on our energy whether they want to or not. There was a way to block that. It would help if I meditated, which wasn't something I did very often. She admitted she had to work on it, too. When I told her I had trouble with concentration, she pointed out that sometimes it helped her to move her body to Native American Music. She said it would be good for me to help refocus my mind and keep my thoughts on track.

21.   I told her how I often felt sick inside, as if I weren't living in my own body. I was paralleling Michael's habits and having thoughts I never had before. Michael had the habit of biting my lip, which was frustrating. At that moment, he started moving my hands. I recounted the story of Michael biting his lip during an interview by Oprah.

104

22.   I told Sandra I was writing the book and lyrics, doing everything Michael asked. My husband asked Sandra what she thought of the situation. She said she knew Michael was there, and I was telling the truth. She predicted his death two days before it happened. She added that Michael really loved me, and our relationship was almost an obsession for him.

23.   I asked Sandra why he loved me so much. I remembered the lyrics he had me write: *I never thought I would be your lover, I never thought I was falling in love with you, this wasn't his plan.* He gave me powerful emotions on a very deep level.

24.   Sandra pointed out that Michael had so much power in his life, and his energy was so strong, that when he visited her at home, none of the fifteen ghosts in her house compared to Michael's energy. I was worried ghosts might follow me home,

but she assured me that wouldn't happen. Michael had a lot of strength, so there was no reason for him to use mine. In his mind, he was totally fixated on me and the past life we shared.

25. Sandra said she had always been a fan of Native- American art and artifacts and had them around her. Michael talked to both of us and told me to put the session with Sandra in the book. He said he liked Sandra.

26. Sandra spoke about the fact that Michael wanted to come out with a song in December. He showed her an image of a town with snow falling on Christmas Eve and children all around.

27. Sandra knew immediately after Michael came to visit that she was supposed to meet with me, but she didn't have my number. I asked how she felt about his energy. She said it wasn't bad, just overpowering and very purple. I understood. That was

how I saw him, too, with a purple aura everywhere.

28.   I told her about seeing a light in my home that was like a blue computer light. The first medium I met told me it was common to see spirits with blue lights around them. Sandra said Michael wasn't finished on earth and had no interest in crossing over yet. I often asked Michael why he didn't want to go to the light, and he said he wasn't ready and wanted to stay awhile. Sandra said the same thing. She pointed out that Michael had no interest in crossing over to the other side and made excuses for staying here. As we all laughed, my husband asked, "Why would he want to stay in this hell?"

29.   I told her Michael wasn't always with me. He went to see his children and other places. Sandra said there was evidence that to those who have passed on, time has no meaning. He could be in his house one second

and be with me the next. Michael called it timeless bliss. He could be everywhere. He told Sandra the same thing.

30. Michael began discussing the lyrics for the Christmas song. He told Sandra it was about the children of the world. Suddenly, I understood. Many children were dying from hunger. It was possible to hear the voices of the forgotten children of the night.

That was the title of the song he guided me to write. Sandra saw him sprinkling snow over a town and also saw Christmas with children. I pointed out that was the song we always listened to, because Michael wanted me to believe the song *Believe* by Josh Groban, from the movie *Polar Express.*

31. Michael wanted fire in his stage show. It was his way to let us know he was around us. My way of connecting with him from the very beginning of our story was through his

eyes. Through his eyes, I had the ability as Lilly to see the world and beyond as Michael did. I felt I could look into his eyes and see the truth. Before a reading, I would look at his picture to reconnect with him and see Beyond the Eyes. His eyes and his vision for the book were my life at that time.

32. The book I was writing excited Michael. Perhaps when it finally was published, it would be a good thing. I was worried about my husband and was frightened about what Michael did to me. I finally told Sandra how

Michael surprised me by using parts of my body. He even woke me up during the night with a song, and I started singing. He moved my hand and told me, "We can feel. This is real." I asked why he took control of my body. He said he had no other choice. I tried many times to stay away from him without success.

33.   Sandra asked him that question, and he said he does those things because he said I was going to do something for him but didn't. I kept asking Michael if I was doing the right thing by writing the book.

34.   Sandra pointed out that most people would believe me and my story. Michael felt I didn't trust him, but he knew what was coming, and I didn't. Michael wanted me to trust him and made a big deal about that. He knew I didn't see the future and wanted me to trust him completely. Sandra said she was a very objective person. It was difficult for her to believe what happened to her, even though her work was validated by the police and others she helped.

35.   When Michael was alive, he was a perfectionist. It felt like I was working for him, which was why he was after me constantly. I feel like him, and Michael needed to understand that he was an energy force, though he took

energy from me at times. He knew he was dead, but he was very focused on me and getting his words and book out.

36. The moment Sandra predicted his death, she knew he wouldn't go easily. He would return and be with us a long time. Even after people said Michael was dead, Sandra knew he would remain on the earth plane. I told her that Michael often said, "I am not dead."

37. My husband pointed out that Michael knew he died, but he wanted to finish his project and be done with the book. Sandra said Michael wasn't going anywhere. He wanted us to know before his death he was in an office with four men wearing suits and sunglasses, trying to make him sign papers for a business deal. Michael stood up and said he didn't want to. He told them to slow down. Whatever happened after that was connected to the meeting.

38. Sandra saw there was something on the table he was ingesting. His neck hurt, and the pain went up through his head. I told her Michael said he had a headache. She felt the pain in his head and neck. He did that to me often, which meant he could give us the same pain he felt before he died.

39. The night he died, he had a really bad headache. He felt dizzy before he slept. He asked Dr. Murray for headache medication. I felt concerned about that part, because I didn't want to blame people. Michael told both of us that the truth would come out about his death. He insisted I was the only one writing a book, and he would not use anybody else.

40. Sandra said everything Michael showed me was true, and he would make everyone else believe it, too. People might think I was crazy, but Michael would give them proof. Michael told me there would be some

people who wouldn't believe me, but most would. It was important for me to trust Michael and keep going through with the project, even if it felt overwhelming at times.

41.   Sandra asked me a funny question. "Do you get out much?" I replied, "Not really." She thought it might be good to go dancing and move my body. Anytime I heard music, I wanted to dance, which was crazy, but it worked. I felt better afterward.

That was the end of our session with Sandra.

Schenatzky

CHAPTER THIRTEEN
Other Spirits

December 4, 2009, after I began writing the book, started out like any other day, but there was a blue glow around the moon. I didn't realize how important it was to protect myself not from Michael but from other negative energies. Every time I saw a medium, I was told to protect myself. I didn't ask what that meant. They told me to surround myself with white light. I soon learned why.

My home had become an open vessel for other spirits to come through besides Michael, and that turned into a big problem. My neighbor across the street died of a heart attack quite suddenly. Within a few days, his spirit came to me and asked me to write a letter to give to his fiancée who still lived in his home.

He said they planned to marry, and his sudden death was a shock to them both. There were things she needed to know. When I said I wasn't interested in doing that for him, he insisted. Finally, I sat down and wrote the letter, then I promptly took it across the street to give to the woman.

The letter told her that the house would be hers, and there was money hidden behind a picture. When I gave her the letter and explained why I was there, she started crying. I told her that her fiancé came to me and insisted I write the letter. She needed to know the house was hers. Since his death was so sudden, he wanted to make sure she was cared for.

The next day, she came over and told me she found the money hidden behind the picture and thanked me for writing the letter.

Other spirits came through me, including a man who died in a car accident who wanted me to tell his family what happened. I felt threatened by those spirits, yet they kept coming. The situation grew worse. I told my husband what was happening, and he said, "This has to stop. You can't do this anymore." I asked the spirits to back off, because I couldn't take it. That was a horrible time.

I promised I'd help Michael, but the more work I did for him, the more spirits came to me. Finally, my husband put me in a hospital one night when I told him I was hearing voices. The doctor put me on medication and left me alone in a room. After I had a CAT scan that didn't show anything abnormal, I was ready to go home. Michael was in the hospital with me, saying it would be OK.

I came home the next day, but the incident at the hospital was very frightening. I didn't understand what was happening to me. The voices kept coming, and so did the lyrics.

Michael gave me the lyrics to "Speechless". I was drinking my morning coffee when he asked me to go onto the computer and check the songs on his web page. "Now I'll show you how I feel," he said.

Everything was there, written in the song he had me write. I was doing what he said, and I was impressed when I saw the song there, just as he said it would be. I never heard of this song before. I was also speechless. I couldn't believe what was happening to me and started crying. I knew I wasn't crazy. My situation grew worse.

My two sisters, who lived in Germany, wanted to visit me in December, 2009. It was Christmas season, and I kept up our tradition of placing a string on the wall to hang Christmas cards. One card had a picture of my sisters. Michael said they were coming to visit, though they'd never been to the United States before.

Two days later, my sister called and said they planned to book a flight in February. We hadn't seen each other in years. Unfortunately, they had to postpone their trip until Spring due to snow. Finally, they booked a flight for April 12, which was significant to me because that also was the anniversary of the date we came to America from Germany. I kept hearing negative voices and felt negative energy around me I couldn't shake. The voices said I would die on April 15.

I didn't want to die. They said if I wanted to be with Michael, I had to die on April 15.

I was terrified of the negative energy. The spirits said I wouldn't be there for my sisters' visit.

My husband thought I was crazy and called the medium to tell her what was happening. She said I needed to protect myself by asking angels to surround me with the white light of divine love. I made a point of doing that each day.

At first it was great having Michael in my life, but it soon changed into a nightmare because of the negative energies. I hadn't protected myself and didn't know how. I felt I was being manipulated by the spirits or voices that told me no one needed me in life.

My sisters arrived on April 12, when I was still being highly manipulated. I needed to talk to one of my sisters. I was so devastated; I told her that I will die soon and that she will be the one who takes care of my children. I felt it was coming soon.

The next morning I woke up. I felt I had enough and took all the medications I had before falling asleep. I didn't know what was happening, but I told my husband that I took all the pills. He immediately called 911.

An ambulance rushed me to the hospital where I was treated and admitted. The doctor told my husband, "If you hadn't acted when you did, she would have died within three hours."

Over the next five days, the physicians gave me different kinds of medication. I still can't remember much about that horrible time.

I was blessed because I survived. It wasn't the time for me to go. It wasn't until later that I realized God wanted me to continue my life and I knew the book was one of the reasons.

CHAPTER FOURTEEN
Conclusion

My gifts to hear, see, and feel Michael Jackson over the past few years has been an amazing experience, positive and negative. It was difficult for my husband, my family, and me. My husband lost interest in hearing about my frequent communications with Michael or other entities and didn't support the completion of this book. I was alone in my spiritual endeavor, which led me to learn more about mediumship.

After completing the book, other unusual things happened. Other entities connected with Michael began communicating with me, too, pretending to be him. Suddenly, I didn't know who had entered my life from the spiritual world.

Since I wasn't sure who was communicating with me, I began to separate myself from the process. I needed to be out of that game. I began to live my life on earth with my family again.

Michael returned one day, frustrated that he was being blocked by the other entities. He didn't like being manipulated by them. He wanted to tell me he was pleased with the book and wanted to be finished with the process. The book needed to be offered to the public.

He said four specific entities were blocking his communications with me. A medium I visited confirmed that. Michael was able to reach her and asked her to contact me, telling her he was being blocked and wouldn't be able to communicate with me anymore

The other entities, however, spoke clearly to me. The medium was able to describe three of them: a girl who passed over as a teenager, a man they called "Baby," and a woman who was deeply in love with him as his soul mate.

Baby described himself as having a lot of power on the other side and had been an American in this life. I heard his name as probably being Don. The two soul mates wished to return to the physical world together. They didn't explain more about why they blocked Michael's communication except to say there was a power struggle between them.

In mid-2012, near the completion of the book, I understood why Michael wanted to disengage himself from contact.

As one medium mentioned previously, when we began the book, Michael had no interest in crossing over into the light and had unfinished business to take care of. Perhaps writing the story he commanded me to finish will give him closure, and he can pass into a higher dimension in the afterlife.

In my last conversation with him, he told me he was moving on. I realized I was a strong channel and decided to offer mediumship classes. My journey opened my eyes to a new world of possibilities, though the chapter of my life with Michael was over.

He understood the difficulties I experienced. In our last conversation, he said, "Keep your head up. Be brave. I have to go on. Please let me go. I can't stay with you forever."

I felt a conflicting sense of sadness and relief at hearing those words. My thoughts and prayers will always be with Michael, an incredibly strong, captivating soul who is missed by the entire world.

CHAPTER FIFTEEN
Addendum

Although I am hesitant to include these words, Michael specifically asked they be in the book. Near the end of the first draft, he communicated these notes to me.

1. Other people were involved in my death. Dr. Murray was the executioner, but it was a framed murder. His actions were purposeful, including not watching the monitor or making 911 calls immediately. I would still be alive if he took action earlier.

2. I was purposely given an overdose of Propofol, and Dr. Murray should have known better. I could still hear noises and voices around me, but I was unable to communicate with him anymore.

3. Since Dr. Murray was a cardiologist, he should have known how to do CPR, yet he did it incorrectly.

4. While I was in serious danger, Dr. Murray was making phone calls.

5. I strongly believe I was murdered by the Illuminati. I warned people about the dangers of the Illuminati on a YouTube video before my death.

6. I want my father to know that his uncaring smile during the interview with TV Guide on June 28, 2009 for his new record company hurt me very much. It was like he didn't acknowledge the seriousness of my death. Because the afterlife is all about love, I have forgiven him.

7. I want to see everything negative on the Internet, TV interviews, and all forms of media be eliminated. I want the pictures and words making fun of me to disappear. Those aren't me, and they aren't the memories I wish to leave the world.

8. More than anything else, I'd like my family, friends, and even those who hurt me in my lifetime to believe this spiritual channeling is accurate. It should be understood as my greatest legacy to the world, along with my music. I had no idea something this important could happen in the afterlife— the ability to channel clearly between dimensions. I'm now ready to pass over to the light.

Schenatzky

CHAPTER SIXTEEN

Lyrics Channeled from Michael to Me

<u>Waiting for You</u>

Remember the things we used to do

The way we fell for each other

The way we stared into each other's eyes

Oh, Baby, I can't wait

I can't wait

Falling for you again

Take me to a place

Where no one has been before

I wanna touch you

Schenatzky

I wanna feel your lips

*I wanna discover a new way to love
you*

Oh, Baby, I can't wait

I can't wait

Falling for you again

*It feels like it takes too long to feel
this
     love again,*

Let me be your obsession

Oh, Baby, I can't wait

I can't wait

Falling for you again

We acted like kids

*Climbing up trees on a beautiful
     summer day*

Beyond The Eyes

We chased each other across the meadow

We watched funny movies and laughed till we fell asleep

I was holding your hands

All I said is, I want you, Baby, I can't wait

Oh, Baby, I can't wait

I can't wait

Falling for you again

When your time on earth is through

I will be there for you

Oh, Baby, I can't wait

I can't wait

Falling for you again

I love you!

Schenatzky

<u>The Way You Love Me</u>

Even though it's been so long

My love for you keeps growing strong

When a feeling gets this strong, you know, Real
 things come along
Fly me up to where you are

I want to feel you by my side

I want to be touched like the very first time

I want to be loved like the very first time

Like we were made for each other

Deep in the stillness I can hear you speak

You are still my inspiration
You're making me believe
 While you're gently sleeping
I hear you inside my dreams

Making me believe that angels can breathe

Beyond The Eyes

I wake up from this dream and make a wish
On a shining star, being together with someone
 like you
I put angel dust in my hand and close my eyes
And blow my wishes away

Our hearts are pounding like one
This is how I feel

Our love will never be torn

Chorus:

The way you love me, I wish it were real
To find this love that I can feel

You belong to me like waves crash on the
 beautiful sea
Our love is combined like a rainbow with
 iridescent colors
I close my eyes, all I can see is your face so
 perfect and so clear
Like a star in the sky which magically appears

You're my inspiration of happiness, every day
 and every night

Schenatzky

You're my everything
Chorus:

The way you love me, I wish it were real
To find this love that I can feel

I wake up my from my dreams and it seems
I will never find someone like you

I cry in tears, I'm in the arms of an angel

That's far away from here

You cover me with feathers under your wings
I can hear you speaking, I will always love you
You must know how much I do.

I'm in a place where time doesn't exist
It is called the timeless Bliss

I open my eyes and I realize I'm back into my life
My thoughtful wishes, written down to make this
Like a poem, if you believe really strong real things will come along

Chorus:

Beyond The Eyes

The way you love me, I wish it were real

To find this love that I can feel

Destiny
<u>(Inspiration January, 2012)</u>

I decided to write this song
Just to let you know exactly the way I feel

Because I love you

I've been waiting for someone like you to make
me feel alive

I'll be right by your side to be your light and
your guide
Just let me reassure you that you can count on
me
It was you, you and me, two hearts drawn
together, bound by destiny
You are my inspirations of all my songs

Chorus
I'm lost in a different world
Then you came in my life

Schenatzky

Our souls were combined
Brought me back to reality
Now I don't need a fantasy
This is our destiny
You are the only one I need

Yeah, Babe, oh

I got down on my knees, and I pleaded with you
I crossed a million oceans just to be with you
I said that I would love you every single night
I swam the longest river just to call your name

Heaven must send me down
Down for you to give me a thrill.
Baby, I'm ready to spend my whole life with you
'Cause I love you

Chorus
I'm lost in a different world
Then you came in my life
Our souls were combined
Brought me back to reality
Now I don't need a fantasy
This is our destiny
You are the only one I need

Beyond The Eyes

Yeah, Babe, oh
That special girl I prayed for every night
Will be my dream and my guide
You're the flame that sets my soul on fire
Every night in our dreams you gave me wings
To make me fly like Peter Pan in the sky
I was blessed to be loved by you

Your eyes are like deep wells of desire
Once in your arms, I'm on fire
You were sent, Girl, so perfectly true
All the love songs I wrote were made for you
Now I'm a survivor in this world, because I
wanna be with you

Chorus
I'm lost in a different world
Then you came in my life
Our souls were combined
Brought me back to reality
Now I don't need a fantasy
This is our destiny
You are the only one I need

Yeah, Babe, oh

Schenatzky

Speechless
(the song Composed by Michael Jackson)

Gone is the craze of expression of passion

To tell you how I feel

But I am speechless

Because that's how you make me feel

<u>Cry</u>
Somebody shakes when the wind blows

Somebody is missing a friend

Hold on

*Somebody is lacking a hero and they have not a
  clue*

Beyond The Eyes

I Need You in My Life

Inspired by Lilly

Let's leave the bad memories behind

So I'll know you'll be fine

I've seen you in tears on the bedroom floor

I need you in my life telling you I can't make it
  without you
I need you in my life in a place where the sun is
  always shining and the sky is always blue

No one understood me, but you do

No one understood my lyrics, but you do
  My life was full of tragedy,
  I tried so hard to put my broken heart together
  again
  And I tell you I can't make it without you
  And I tell you I can't make it without you

It's hard to breathe when your soul gets lost
This is why I love you the most

Schenatzky

I'm stuck in the middle of nowhere, a place with
No name, I'm not strong enough to make it
 through
Without you, I need to go on, but I can't make it
 without you

Chorus
I need you in my life where the sun is
always shining and the sky is always blue
It's just a matter of time

My life on Earth is over and done
I left my work, my everything behind
Heaven can wait until you're mine
I can't make it without you I can't make it
 without you
Oh, yeah

Chorus

I need you in my life where the sun is always
 shining and the sky is always blue
It's just a matter of time

It's hard to breathe when your soul gets lost
This is why I love you the most
I'm stuck in the middle of nowhere, a place

With no name, I'm not strong enough to make it
  through
Without you

Chorus
I need you in my life where the sun is always
  shining and the sky is always blue
It's just a matter of time

I can't make it without you

I can't make it without you

Oh, yeah

Let's leave the bad memories behind
So I'll know you'll be fine
I've seen you in tears on the bedroom floor
I keep telling you I can't make it without you
I need you in my life in a place where the sun is
  always shining and the sky is always blue

<u>*Believe*</u>

It is just a dream? Heaven to my heart

Schenatzky

It is always an inner voice that says

I have chosen you to be loved

You are the one

I searched for you all of my life

It feels like I've known you a thousand years
I've seen your light
It was shining so bright

Chorus
Wanted you to get addicted with your eyes
Wanted you to believe
Wanted you to fall in love with me
Wanted it to become a true story—oh, yeah

I said I will go this way together with you
And I will listen to you and do what your heart
 desires
And I realize I can't talk to anybody

And I have to live with this myself

I gave you my heart

Beyond The Eyes

With all my love
I never thought that you would be my lover

Chorus
Wanted you to get addicted with your eyes
Wanted you to believe
Wanted you to fall in love with me
Wanted it to become a true story—oh, yeah

Thousand times I kissed you in my dreams
How can it be? Falling in love with you? You
 (Michael) said, "I prayed in hope of
finding you, the love I was searching for"

(Line written in Michael 's song Another
Day)

 The Mortality is a mystery

Of timeless bliss this moment of now

(My planet earth poem)

(He knew he was going to die soon)

Schenatzky

But we can feel this is real
Doesn't it blow your mind away?
This is our story
And we know it's true—oh, yeah

Chorus
Wanted you to get addicted with your eyes
Wanted you to believe
Wanted you to fall in love with me
Wanted it to become a true story—oh, yeah

Lilly writing Lyrics

CHAPTER SEVENTEEN
Letters

Sent to the Michael Jackson Foundation on 1/25/2012:

To Latoya (and the same letter sent to Janet)

I write this letter with great reluctance because of how it might impact you and possibly change your interpretations of certain events. This may provoke pain, fear, and/or misunderstanding, all of which I would rather avoid. I'm only interested in informing you of the events that have unfolded in my life and the impact they had in my life. I write this out of respect for you and my desire to provide you with advance notice.

I am not interested in pursuing any merits, blessings, or commitments in any way from you. I wish to provide you my testimony and the actions I am taking based on these events. My purpose is to merely inform you of this information, so you may prepare for potential reactions to the outcomes. I write this out of respect for you and my desire to provide you with advance notice.

I have been asked to write you this letter on behalf of a very, very dear spirit to you and me. I know you may find this hard to believe and/or understand, but for some reason, I have been called forth to provide a message on a grand scale.

I even question myself as to why would I have been chosen or provided the gift to bring forward this message. I am no one special but for some reason have been provided an opportunity to connect with the spirit's information. As a child, I had no connection with this person, nor did I closely follow this person, yet I have access to their message.

I have even visited mediums to ask these same questions, and they have confirmed that I am connecting to information provided directly by this specific spirit. I provided no details to the mediums, yet they told me the name of the person and provided information about us that I was unaware of.

Again, the only reason I am writing you is because Michael asked that I contact you. If he hadn't asked, you would not be receiving this. I am sorry to be the one, but Michael believed it to be important, as I carry his message forward.

You know that Michael had special gifts and grandiose visions for the world and life on earth. He wanted all of us to be one, to join in his vision in harmony and to keep on living. He wanted us to be free and to create a world worth living in.

Well, he still wants the world to know, and he won't leave until we do.

Michael has been a guide to millions of people, showing them a way of living.

He wanted to raise the awareness, to create a vision, to take a stand for what is right.

He wanted us to be a source for a world of love, to live through love.

To live every day through love in every way! Make a better world!

Michael has created lyrics for songs which I have written to be shared with you. He asked that these lyrics be included with this letter. I believe that he is communicating his vision for the world and his desire for us as human beings.

He would love to watch us live through love. And in doing so, we show our love for him.

I have also been asked to write a book about Michael and my connection to him through the information he has provided in the spiritual realm. I would not be doing so if I hadn't been asked. Michael wants this information shared with the world, so he can continue to inspire his vision from above.

And with that, I am enclosing the introduction from the book This Is It, a true story about Michael Jackson and Lilly.

Beyond The Eyes

In spiritual bliss and peace,

Sylvia Schenatzky

████████████

██████████████████

www.thisisitlilly.com

Schenatzky

CHAPTER EIGHTEEN
Mediums

I thought it would be appropriate to explore and share information about the possibilities of communicating with spirits. Mediums claim they can speak with the spirits of those who have passed on. This can be done in a variety of ways, as some mediums receive thoughts from a spirit, while at other times, they are presented with mental images. Then again, some mediums actually hear spirit voices.

Many mediums describe receiving their first spirit communication at a very young age, which, as might be imagined, makes for a rather difficult childhood. As children, we are much more open to these communications. Some parents try to squelch these visions and unusual commentaries.

If the gift is passed down from generation to generation, then it meets with encouragement, rather than discouragement, as in the case of the popular medium Sylvia Brown. Her grandmother was instrumental in assuring her she wasn't going crazy and helped her handle her gift properly. Sylvia wrote many books to educate people about her amazing gift and candidly shares her life experiences.

James Van Pragh expresses his belief that there is no such thing as death. Even though the body ceases to function, the soul lives on. It is these souls with whom he communicates. His communication takes place after people have crossed over into the light.

He wrote Talking to Heaven, Reaching to Heaven, and Ghosts Among Us. He starred in his own TV show, "Beyond with James Van Pragh" and is the coexecutive producer of the TV hit series, "Ghost Whisperer".

That show is based on the life of medium Mary Ann Winkowski, who also began communicating with spirits at an early age. The difference between her and Van Pragh is that James communicates with spirits after they cross over, while Mary Ann communicates with spirits that are known as earthbound and haven't yet gone into the light.

The TV series reflects that fact that some spirits stay behind out of fear of the unknown or because they feel the need to take care of unfinished business. Mary Ann is able to help such spirits resolve their conflicts and find the light, so they can cross over as depicted in "Ghost Whisperer".

As with any talent, some mediums are able to communicate with those who have gone into the light, while others have the ability to communicate with those who are earthbound. The importance of the talent is that it brings tremendous comfort to those who have lost loved ones and helps confirm that souls live on after death, as in Michael Jackson's case. Michael had no interest in crossing over, because he wanted to watch his kids and make sure their lives went well by helping influence events.

Yes, I lived this this experience at Michael's direction. He could manipulate my dreams and told me exactly what I would see. I dreamed it as he told me. When I asked him how that worked, he said, "When the time's right, I'll tell you."

When people visit a medium, the medium has no control over who comes through. That's entirely up to the spirit. Visitors should go to a session with open minds and refrain from giving up too much information. They should let the medium supply the information, then the visitor can validate it.

For many reasons, people who have recently died sometimes remain in the earthly plane for a while before cutting their ties and crossing over to the other side. Many psychics and mediums can welcome them to the light and bless them. They tell such spirits that they are free from fear and pain, forgiven, and will be welcomed into the light. They then call upon their own highest nature or guardian angel to ask them to accompany the spirit into the light, taking them to their rightful place in the universe and releasing their attachment to the earth plane, cutting the cord to anyone still alive.

Such spirits often sound fearful about crossing over. One way to help them is to teach them what awaits them on the other side. Some people are so frightened of judgment that they choose to stay between worlds to avoid going to hell. Once they know there's nothing to fear, that only love awaits them, they decide to go.

Another type of soul who is stuck here are those who wait for a loved one or have unfinished business. They don't experience time, and they may believe they are still alive or still living on earth time. Several mediums I visited said that Michael was still here with unfinished business to complete. With that kind of crossing, the spirit must be convinced he is dead and that his loved ones have crossed over and are waiting for him on the other side.

Psychics and mediums share with their clients the importance of facing fear and transforming that into empathy. Psychics help spirits cross over in various ways, but it's mostly through communication.

One example of that was shared by a medium. The incident happened three years earlier when she began getting scary vibes from a corner of her basement. It was so cold and prickly down there, even her friends mentioned it if they went downstairs.

One day, she had enough of that scary thing trying to frighten her out of her own basement, so she turned to confront it and tried to hide her fear. She looked directly at the corner, thinking she would see a monster, but it was only a pale, bald, little boy in a hospital gown.

She realized he'd been a cancer patient at the local hospital, where he died. He told her that he ran down a tunnel and took up residence in her basement, hiding from the nurses and his mother. He didn't trust those on the other side to escort him to the afterlife.

"They'll turn me into a pin cushion again," he said. He felt his medical treatment was horrible, and he died frightened and distrustful of everyone and everything.

The medium's fear turned to compassion. She was finally able to convince him to trust her. She told him he died, that he was finished with medical treatments, and he had to go with the angels. After twenty minutes, he left gently, taking the cold, prickly energy with him. She never saw him again.

Sometimes, all it takes to help someone cross over is a simple conversation. The medium recalled how terrified she was when she decided to confront the energy. Mediums and psychics talk to the dead all the time, but not all are brave.

CHAPTER NINETEEN
Auras

Auras are best described as energy fields that are our life force surrounding our bodies. Aura readings date back to ancient times, most notably by Buddhists, Hindus, Greeks, and Romans, who could generally see the first three layers of auras closest to the body, which signify the mind, emotions, and health. The outer layers signify the soul and spirit.

Many describe seeing auras around people as resembling heat radiating in a variety of colors. The layer closest to the body is known as the etheric layer and is a bluish-white color, indicating the person's health and well-being. The second layer relates to emotions and feelings and is connected to the second

KETHERIC BODY
(mental aspect)

CELESTIAL BODY
(emotional aspect)

ETHERIC TEMPLATE
(physical aspect)

ASTRAL BODY

MENTAL BODY
(lower
mental aspect)

EMOTIONAL BODY
(lower
emotional aspect)

ETHERIC BODY
(lower
etheric aspect)

*The Seven Layer
Auric Body System*

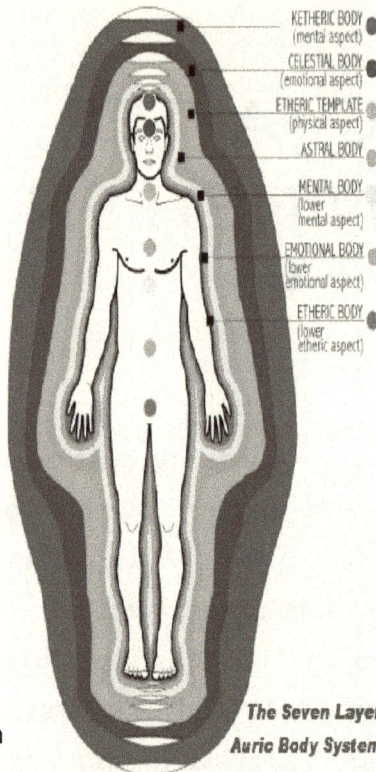

chakra, which changes constantly depending on the person's mood. It can also reveal any past, painful emotions, or fears. If someone's emotions are blocked, this layer can show dark areas. It is usually characterized by a variety of colors emanating from one to six inches from the body.

The mental aura, the third layer, is connected to people's consciousness, intellect, and ideas, showing the state of someone's mental health. It usually gives off a bright-yellow color from three to eight inches around the head. If someone is in deep thought or concentration, the color is more intense.

Spirit is located in the fourth layer and gives off a beautiful array of colors eight to twelve inches from the body. This layer is connected to the heart chakra, focusing on love. If a person is well-loved, this will show shades of pink or rose.

The fifth layer, the spiritual, glows with a brilliant blue light. It is related to the throat chakra, focusing on communication creativity, holding higher aspects of the will in higher consciousness.

The celestial layer is the sixth layer, giving off an array of pastel, iridescent threads of light two to three feet from the body. This layer relates to dreams and memories. It reflects the subconscious mind and is connected to the brow chakra. This layer shows the spirit's emotional layer and is where the physical mind connects with the spiritual mind.

The last layer is connected to the crown chakra and relates to the higher mind, connecting with divine spiritual awareness. It is golden-white in color and emanated three to five feet from the body. It holds all the other aura layers together.

People may have heard the terms "green with envy," or, "I'm feeling blue," which are based on aura colors. If a psychic or medium is gifted enough to identify different aura colors or a specific color around a person, the medium can help people release emotional baggage or live the life he or she wants. Someone dealing with depression might have dark-blue areas in his aura. If he is angry or hot-tempered, he might have red around his physical body.

I was able to see Michael's aura, which was best described as royal purple.

He told me he would wake me at three o'clock in the morning so I could see him in the dark. He did it four times, which surprised and excited me when I saw him surrounded by a beautiful purple color.

Aura colors around people indicate a lot about their personality and give information about their future. Psychics and mediums can detect predominant aura colors. The ability can be taught to those who are interested.

Generally, people surrounded by purple are highly psychic, extremely sensitive, and in tune with other people's emotions.

They are known to be mysterious and rather secretive, which many who knew Michael would confirm. A purple aura also signifies a curious, philosophical mind that is also intuitive. Such people never stop exploring or learning new areas of interest, which makes them interesting people who usually become known for their knowledge of many topics.

They may not have many friends, because they prefer a more-isolated life, but the friends they have will be very close, well- respected, greatly admired, and loved. It's difficult for such people to find a perfect mate. One he does, he will be committed for life and will be extremely loyal.

Michael adored animals, which is another common trait of people with purple auras. Such people also spend time with nature. They can sense animals' emotions and feelings. People surrounded by purple auras have an "open-door" policy, always taking in and caring for strangers, which Michael did often for seriously ill children.

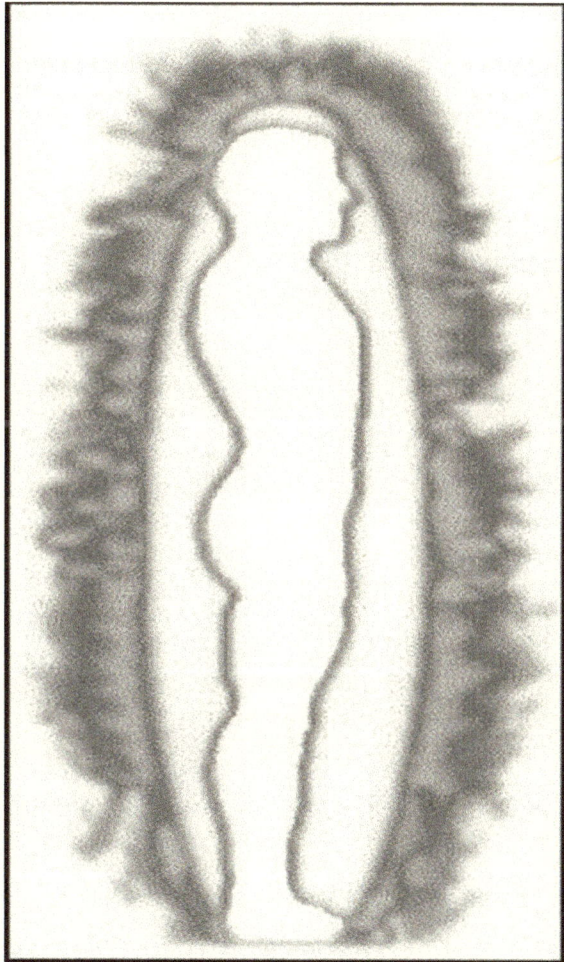

Schenatzky

About the Author
Sylvia Schenatzky

Sylvia was born and raised in Germany and noticed her gift at nine years of age. She surprised her parents and siblings with her ability to know things before they happened, which most of her family would have rather ignored.

Sylvia always wanted to live in the United States and moved there from Germany in 2003 after a long, difficult time with immigration. She is a proud American who lives with her husband and two children in Florida.

Her experience with Michael Jackson was incredibly difficult and overwhelming at times. She works hard to stay healthy and strong. It is her hope that her book will give people hope and will tell those with a similar gift that they aren't alone.

Schenatzky

Write to Sylvia at
sylviaschenatzky@hotmail.com or visit
www.thisisitlilly.com.

About the Illustrator
Kate Johannsen

Award-winning artist Kate Johannsen was discovered by Udo and Sylvia Schenatzky when they searched the Internet for art lessons for one of their daughters. Kate and her husband, Jim Johannsen, own Brush and Shutter Studio Gallery, where Kate is the brush, and photographer Jim is the shutter. Sylvia and Udo gazed around the gallery at Kate and Jim's beautiful creations while their daughter cleaned up after her art lessons.

Kate likes working in a variety of mediums (oil, acrylic, watercolor, pastels, colored pencil, and more), but it was Kate's graphite pencil drawings that enticed Sylvia the most. Kate's artwork ranges from the light and whimsical to the serious. Many have an almost-obsessive photographic accuracy. Kate creates Pet Portraits with such incredible detail that it is possible to see the animal's individual hairs. Customers rave about her work and keep coming back for portraits of other pets. And yes, Kate does people portraits, too.

See more of Kate Johannsen's work at www.brushnshutter.com or contact her at brushandshutter@earthlink.net.

The All Seeing Power
• and the All Seeing Eye •

This message was delivered
from Michael to me
to understand and release
it to the world.

Sylvia Shenabby
known by 2;00